YO-BZZ-718

631.2
Mil

GETTING THE JOB DONE

COMMERCIAL FISHERS

Nathan Miloszewski

PowerKiDS
press

New York

Published in 2020 by The Rosen Publishing Group, Inc.
29 East 21st Street, New York, NY 10010

First Edition

Editor: Greg Roza
Book Design: Reann Nye

Photo Credits: Cover Charles C. Place/Getty Images; p. 5 Monty Rakusen/Cultura/Getty Images; p. 6 Jorge Manso/Shutterstock.com; pp. 7, 20 John Wollwerth/Shutterstock.com; p. 9 Library of Congress/Getty Images; p. 10 ALPA PROD/Shutterstock.com; p. 11 Boston Globe/Getty Images; p. 13 Adrian Peacock/DigitalVision/Getty Images; p. 14 Clifford Wayne Estes/Shutterstock.com; p. 15 stockfour/Shutterstock.com; p. 17 Portra/DigitalVision/Getty Images; p. 19 Portland Press Herald/Getty Images; p. 21 positive emotions/Shutterstock.com; p. 22 Victoria Kurylo/Shutterstock.com.

Library of Congress Cataloging-in-Publication Data

Names: Miloszewski, Nathan, author.
Title: Commercial fishers / Nathan Miloszewski.
Description: New York : PowerKids Press, [2020] | Series: Getting the job done | Includes index.
Identifiers: LCCN 2019000947| ISBN 9781725301245 (pbk.) | ISBN 9781725301269
 (library bound) | ISBN 9781725301252 (6 pack)
Subjects: LCSH: Fisheries–Vocational guidance–Juvenile literature. | Fishers–Juvenile literature.
Classification: LCC SH331.9 .M55 2020 | DDC 639.2023–dc23
LC record available at https://lccn.loc.gov/2019000947

Manufactured in the United States of America

CPSIA Compliance Information: Batch #CSPK19. For Further Information contact Rosen Publishing, New York, New York at 1-800-237-9932.

CONTENTS

WHERE DO YOUR FISH STICKS COME FROM?

If you've ever gone fishing at a lake, river, or stream, you know how hard it can be sometimes to catch just one fish. Think about how much time it would take to catch enough to feed your family, all the people who live on your street, or even all the people who live in your city or town!

Have you ever wondered where the fish sticks in your freezer, the fresh fish in your local supermarket, or the lobsters you see swimming in a tank at a restaurant come from? A dirty and dangerous job called commercial fishing helps bring this food to our local grocery stores and restaurants.

A commercial fisherman uses a big net to catch fish from the ocean. >

5

GET YOUR START AS A DECKHAND

Commercial fishers are people who catch fish for money. Fishermen and fisherwomen generally get their start as a deckhand, the lowest-ranking member on a fishing boat.

Fascinating Career Facts

After the fish are caught, they have to be cleaned and stored so that they don't go bad. Just like at home, fish caught at sea have to be refrigerated or placed in ice in storage areas below deck.

Deckhands haul in a full fishing net. They'll measure, clean, sort, and store these fish until they get back to port, where they'll then unload their catch.

The fishing boat captain is the boss who makes sure that the boat is **seaworthy**, that there's enough food and supplies to last the trip, and that all the **equipment** is working.

Once at sea, fish are caught with nets, lines, and traps. Machinery is used to **hoist** the fish onto the boat. The fish are measured and looked at. If a fish is too small, injured, or sick, it is released back into the water.

ONE OF THE OLDEST JOBS

Commercial fishing is one of the oldest jobs, dating back to early **civilization**. Large piles of fish remains have been found all over the world at ancient settlements that are near sources of water.

People used traps and nets to catch fish near the shore. As technology improved, boats and other equipment were used to go further out into deeper water to catch larger amounts of fish to sell to larger populations of people.

Today, commercial fishing businesses come in all different sizes. Some are big, while others are small, family-run businesses. Most use large boats and machines to haul in their catch.

Early methods of fishing were as simple as using a spear to catch fish from the shore.

>

9

LIVING ON A FISHING BOAT

When you work on a fishing boat, you also live there. You're on the boat for days, weeks, or months at a time before coming back into port. You need to be prepared for long days, hard work, and not a lot of sleep.

Fascinating Career Facts

Most fishing jobs are seasonal and only available during the summer. This schedule works for teachers, college students, or other workers who are off during this time.

The crew has a limited amount of time to relax. The living area on a commerical fishing boat is very small. There's not a lot of room, so crew members have to make **efficient** use of space for everything on the boat, including equipment, storage for the caught fish, and food storage for the crew.

11

BIG WAVES, DANGEROUS WORK, AND NO DAYS OFF

In the United States, commercial fishers in Alaska work in some of the most dangerous conditions in the world. Workers in the salmon **fishery** have the highest number of deaths, with around 12 deaths per year.

The weather makes this demanding work even harder, causing large waves to hit the boat. The boat can sink, turn over, or run into rocks.

Because the boat is always wet and moving from side to side, crew members can slip on the deck, lose their balance, fall overboard, and drown. Other reported deaths happen from injuries, or from getting tangled in the nets or hit by other equipment.

Fascinating Career Facts

The number one goal of any commercial fishing boat is to make money, so there are no days off during the season. Crew members generally work seven days a week with no time off to **maximize** the money they make.

Working in the dark, battling large waves, and keeping your balance on deck are some of the challenges of being a commercial fisher.

FLOATING FISH FACTORY

Blood, guts, and the smell of dead, rotting fish—if those things don't bother you, then commercial fishing might be the right job for you.

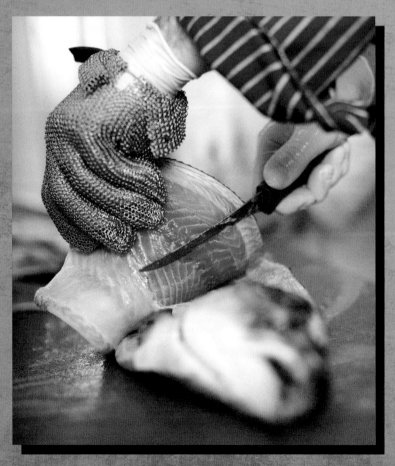

The largest fishing ships are known as floating fish factories because they catch fish and prepare them for sale all on the same boat. A factory boat is where you'll find the most disgusting parts of the job.

These ships have processing lines to turn the fish into fillets that people eat. After processing, the fish are packed up and frozen in storage areas with low temperatures—about –20°Fahrenheit (–29°Celsius).

FROM WATER TO STORE

Factory ships are very **mechanized**, with moving belts and other equipment to move fish from one station to another. As a fish comes down the line, the first step is to drain it by using a knife. The liquids can shoot out all over and you might get it in your face, eyes, or mouth!

Next, you clean the fish of everything except the meat that is eaten. Finally, you'll move the wet, slimy fish into trays so that they can be frozen. Once frozen, they get bagged up to offload and sell.

Fascinating Career Facts

If the fish stop moving on the belts, you'll need to go into the fish storage tank and shovel them onto the processing line. The smell can be **overwhelming**.

The Unted States, Russia, and Japan have large fleets of factory ships.

LEARNING ON THE JOB

One of the great things about becoming a commercial fisher is that you don't need special training or a college degree. You can learn on the job and start at the bottom as a deckhand, then work your way up.

If you don't have much experience fishing, it can help to get **vocational** training with an **internship** at a fishery or on a fishing boat. This training teaches you about fish, the environment, and different fish products.

It's also important to learn about fishing technology such as the tools, **navigation** equipment, nets, and ropes that you'll use every day working on a boat.

Fascinating Career Facts

To become a captain of the largest commercial fishing boats, you need to go through training that's approved by the U.S. Coast Guard and get a commercial fishing license.

Commercial fishers wear special waterproof suits and get safety and survival training in case they have to jump ship during an emergency. These suits help keep them warm and dry in cold water.

WHY BECOME A COMMERCIAL FISHER?

Commercial fishing could be a good career choice if you're someone who loves the outdoors and likes to work with your hands. The dangers and challenges of living and working on a commerical fishing boat may excite you.

Fascinating Career Facts

It's possible to work as a deckhand on a boat before becoming a commercial fisher. You can make more money as your skills and experience grow.

If you aren't fond of life on a fishing boat, the commercial fishing industry has other jobs, such as fishmonger—or someone who prepares and sells raw fish.

Not everyone goes to college and works a desk job. With fishing, you'll have an office that is like nothing else on land. Another benefit is the pay. The average commercial fisher can make more than $36,000 per year. However, since the work is seasonal, they make that much or more in a few short months, leaving them free to work other jobs during the year.

THE FUTURE OF FISHING

The number of fishing jobs may go down in the future because of new laws that limit certain types of fishing, **environmental** concerns such as pollution that harm fish, and new technology and machines that can replace the need for workers. The demand for seafood isn't going down, though. There is still a need for commercial fishers to go out and catch this important food source.

There are always workers who try it for a season and don't come back. If you want to fish for a living, you'll likely have no problem finding a job and taking the place of someone who found out that the job wasn't right for them. Is commercial fishing a career for you?

GLOSSARY

civilization: An advanced society.

efficient: Capable of getting the results you want without wasting time and effort.

environmental: Having to do with the natural world.

equipment: Supplies or tools needed for a certain purpose.

fishery: The business of fishing or a place that catches fish.

hoist: To raise up, lift, or use a machine to move heavy objects.

internship: The act of a student learning by working with experienced professionals.

maximize: Making the most of something, increasing to the highest amount.

mechanize: To switch to a process that uses machinery to do things automatically without the help of humans.

navigation: The act or process of finding the way to get to a place when you are traveling.

overwhelming: Too strong to deal with.

seaworthy: Safe for traveling on the sea or any body of water.

vocational: Relating to or undergoing training in a skill or trade to be pursued as a career.

INDEX

WEBSITES

Due to the changing nature of Internet links, PowerKids Press has developed an online list of websites related to the subject of this book. This site is updated regularly. Please use this link to access the list: www.powerkidslinks.com/GTJD/fishers